The Barcode Blueprint

EVOLUTION AND IMPACT ON
SUPPLY CHAIN

Abdul-Rahim Iddrisu

ISBN: 9798320967363

Contact the Author
Email: iabdulrahim9@gmail.com
Tel: +233240471683

Contents

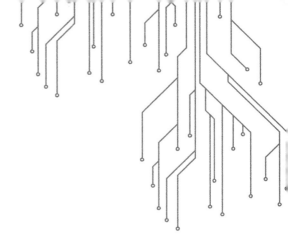

Dedication

Acknowledgement

Introduction to the Concept of Barcodes_____1

The History & Evolution of Barcodes_____5

Clarifying Common Misconceptions on Retail
Barcodes_____17

Barcodes for the Novice Producer & How it Can
Benefit Them_____29

The Role of Barcodes in Supply Chain Management_____35

Book Barcodes & Identifiers Including Magazines,
Periodicals & Music – ISBN/ISSN/ISMN_____43

Barcode-Based Loyalty Programs_____49

Barcodes and E-commerce_____53

Decoding the Scan_____61

Beyond Retail: Applications of Barcodes in
Other Industries_____75

The Future of Barcodes and Emerging Barcode
Technologies: A Crystal Ball for Novice Business Owners____85

1.

Introduction To The Concept Of Barcodes

A barcode refers to a visual representation of data in the form of a series of black and white bars and spaces. Barcodes are designed to be read by barcode scanners or readers, which interpret the pattern and decode the information encoded in the barcode. The information to be encoded in a barcode can represent various types of data, such as product identifiers, pricing information, or tracking numbers. Barcodes are used in retail, logistics, and other industries to facilitate accurate data capture, streamline processes, and enhance efficiency. A barcode is therefore an image used to represent a set of numbers or other characters which can then be easily read by a barcode scanner or cell phone app.

Recognising what a barcode is:
Barcodes can manifest in different forms depending

on the symbology used and the specific requirements of the application. Below write-up gives a brief overview of some common forms of barcodes. An elaboration is made at a later chapter on each type.

1. Linear Barcodes

These barcodes consist of a series of parallel bars and spaces of varying widths. Examples of linear barcodes include the Universal Product Code (UPC), the European Article Number (EAN) and the Interleaved Two of Five (ITF) barcodes. Linear barcodes encode data in a horizontal format.

2. 2D Barcodes (Data Matrix & Stacked)

i. Data Matrix: Unlike linear barcodes, 2D Data Matrix barcodes contain data in both the horizontal and vertical dimensions. They typically appear as square or rectangular patterns composed of small black and white modules (in its original form). Examples of 2D Matrix barcodes include Quick Response (QR) codes and Data Matrix codes. These barcodes store significantly more data than linear barcodes and are capable of encoding text, URLs, or even entire documents and images.

Data Matrix Code   **QR Code**

Data matrix images can store alphanumeric data of up to 2,335 and QR code can store similar data of up to 4,296 characters.

Whiles both are 2D barcodes that encodes data in black and white, or contrasting dark and light, cells arranged in a grid, they are also omnidirectional, meaning that they can be read from any angle. In terms of sizes, QR codes are bigger than Data matrix codes but they are both 2D symbology barcodes.

ii. Stacked Barcodes: Stacked barcodes are a form of 2D that is composed of multiple rows of linear barcode symbols stacked on top of each other. This allows for more data to be encoded within a smaller space. Examples of stacked barcodes include PDF417 and Code 128 stacked barcodes. The stacked barcodes belong to the data bar family that are represented by seven different symbologies. Four of these can be used in retail at the Point of Sale whilst the other three are used in other industries. Although not common, I have presented sample images below of how this category of barcodes looks like.

(01) 0 9501101 53000 3

(01) 0 9501101 53000 3

3. Customized Barcodes

In some cases, barcodes can be customized to meet specific requirements. This may involve altering the shape, size, or style of the barcode to fit particular applications or design preferences. Customized barcodes can be used for branding purposes or to incorporate additional visual elements alongside the encoded data. Irrespective of the extent of customization of a barcode, its data reading pattern will still align with one of the above forms, making a customized barcode an extension of 2D, Linear or within the Data bar family of symbologies. Few examples of customised barcodes are as follows.

2.

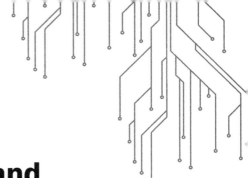

The History and Evolution of Barcodes

Let's delves into the fascinating history and evolution of barcodes, tracing the origins and the pivotal milestones that led to their widespread adoption in the retail industry, the introduction of concepts such as the bullseye barcode and the development of the Universal Product Code (UPC).

I will not also forget to highlights the impact of the barcode revolution on retail operations, the subsequent growth in efficiency, accuracy, and the technological advancements that have shaped the barcode systems over time, including the transition from traditional linear barcodes to more versatile two-dimensional barcodes like QR codes.

From Early Concepts to Widespread Adoption
Barcodes dates back to the 1940s when a graduate student named Bernard Silver and a

food chain executive named Norman Joseph Woodland conceived the idea of a system that could automatically capture product information at the checkout counter. This led to the invention of the bullseye barcode, a circular pattern of concentric circles, which could be scanned using ultraviolet light. However, the bullseye barcode faced technological limitations and was not widely adopted.

The traction on barcodes was massive in the 1970s with the development of the Universal Product Code (UPC). The UPC, developed by George J. Laurer and his team at IBM, introduced the rectangular barcode format that we are familiar with today. The first product to bear a UPC barcode was a pack of Wrigley's chewing gum, scanned on June 26, 1974, in a Marsh Supermarket in Ohio.

Hopefully in future the evolution may cause retailers to celebrate June 26 as the first scan day which has since giving rise to billions of scans daily across the globe.

It has become a universal system for keeping track of items and prices in inventory systems worldwide. Barcodes are now used by almost all retailers worldwide. The system works with the premise that each barcode is only allocated to one product, and therefore in any store, there is no chance of a barcode being on two different products. This system incorporates both UPC-A numbers and the superset EAN-13 Numbers.

The Impact of Barcodes on Retail Operations

The adoption of barcodes has brought a revolutionary change in retail operations. With the ability to quickly and accurately scan barcodes, retailers automate processes that were once labour-intensive and error-prone. The checkout process has become faster, more efficient, and less reliant on manual data entry. Retailers can now track inventory levels in real-time, streamline reordering processes, and gain valuable insights into sales trends and consumer behaviour.

Barcodes enable accurate pricing and inventory control. Gone were the days of manually labelling and changing prices on individual products. The barcode's unique identifier now allow retailers to easily access product information, pricing details, and promotions, ensuring accurate pricing at the point of sale. Inventory management has become more streamlined, with the ability to track stock levels, monitor expiration dates, and identify slow-moving or out-of-stock items. Barcodes software or POS software have extensions that enables the full utilization of this feature. There are off-the-shelve packages and in-house packages that can be used by each business.

Technological Advancements and Barcode Types

Over the years, barcode technology has continued to evolve, introducing new barcode types and encoding methods. While the Universal Product Code (UPC) remains the most widely used barcode system in North America, the European Article Number (EAN) system gained popularity in Europe, Africa and many other parts of the world. These barcodes enabled global trade and facilitate the seamless movement of goods across borders.

Beyond linear barcodes like UPC and EAN, the two-dimensional barcodes, such as QR codes, emerged as versatile tools for information storage. QR codes could contain large amounts of data, including text, URLs, and multimedia content. They quickly gained popularity for marketing campaigns, ticketing systems, and contactless payments.

Currently in Ghana, the government is using the QR system in enabling cashless payment systems across many government offices and departments including payment of taxes to the central government.

Understanding the Barcode Technology

I will concentrate on barcode technology, covering various aspects such as barcode types, encoding methods, and symbologies. An added write-up will be on the structure of barcodes, exploring the arrangement of bars and spaces and how they represent information.

After a brief look at the different barcode symbologies, including UPC, EAN, and QR codes, and their specific applications in the retail industry, I will conclude the section by looking at the significance of barcode scanners and readers.

Barcode Structure and Composition

Barcodes consist of a series of black and white bars of varying widths, along with quiet zones on either side that help scanners identify the beginning and end of the barcode. The arrangement of these bars and spaces follows specific patterns that represent different characters or digits. The bars and spaces in a barcode are designed to be read by a barcode scanner or reader, which interprets the pattern and decodes the information embedded in the barcode. With or without the numbers around the barcodes, especially in the case of UPC and EAN, the barcodes line will still get decoded by a scanner or an app designed for that purpose.

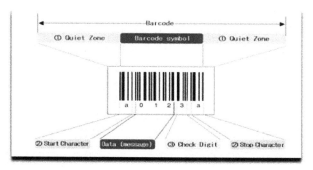

Image credit: denso-wave

Types of Barcodes

Barcode symbologies are standard in the form of Linear, 2D or the Data bar range and usage may depend on the industry of interest.

The Universal Product Code (UPC) is widely utilized in North America and is primarily associated with retail products. UPC barcodes encode a unique product identifier, such as a SKU or GTIN (Global Trade Item Number), allowing for accurate product identification and pricing.

The European Article Number (EAN) system is similar to UPC but is more prevalent in Europe, Africa and many other parts of the world. EAN barcodes also encode product information and serve as an identifier for retail products. It is mostly a 13 digit barcode number that converts to an image in multiple file types. For producers targeting places other than America and Canada, this is the suitable barcode for your products.

Both the UPC and the EAN can be used to generate a carton barcode in multiples. This is the ITF-14 carton barcode and is purposely for cartons or boxes containing individual products with the original UPC or EAN barcode. For instance, about 10 unique ITF-14 barcodes numbers can be generated using an EAN-13 barcode. This is to ensure that the carton barcodes have some similarity with the product barcodes in the boxes.

Another significant advancement in barcode technology is the two-dimensional (2D) barcode. The most prominent example of a 2D barcode is the Quick Response (QR) code. QR codes consist of a square matrix of black and white modules that can store significantly more data than linear barcodes. They are commonly used for various applications beyond product identification, including marketing campaigns, mobile payments, and digital content sharing. QR codes are a phenomenal introduction in the barcodes industry. There is the static/generic QR codes and a dynamic QR codes. The former requires no internet connectivity to scan. An app is enough to get the encoded message decoded for the user. A little of customization can be applied in terms of colour, shapes and the design. Static/Regular QR can be purchased in a one-time transaction for a life time. For regular QR, one QR has to be created for one function at a time. For instance, there can be a QR for a URL, Text, email, Phone, vcard, location; social media handles like facebook, twitter. It is important to use One QR for one purpose.

Dynamic QR codes require internet connectivity to have a full scan and can be monitored on a unique dashboard that comes along with the purchase transaction. The locations of the scans can be tracked, the devices used can be identified and the exact times of the scans can be seen. Massive customizations can be done on dynamic QR codes including automatic generations using API configurations. For all these features, dynamic QR codes are subscription based and not a one-off or life time purchase. A Dynamic QR can be acquired for a project and will expire at the end of the specified time. Any subsequent scan will return negative results as unreachable.

In Ghana, all the above mentioned retail barcodes can be acquired at www.barcodesghana.com, an online platform noted for genuine barcodes. Producers from other countries can check their local spaces or contact *www.internationalbarcodes.net* for local URLs where retail barcodes can be acquired in small quantities without annual subscriptions.

Encoding Methods and Symbologies

Barcode encoding methods determine how data is represented within the bars and spaces of a barcode. Different encoding methods accommodate various types of data, including numerical digits, alphanumeric characters, and binary data. Common encoding methods include Numeric-Only, Alphanumeric, and Byte. This is done with the use of computer software or a POS package especially at the retail space. For this reason, all such POS software has extensions to update product details which include the barcode details.

Barcode symbologies define the rules and structure for encoding data within barcodes. Examples of popular symbologies include Code 39, Code 128, Data Matrix, QR code, Aztec and PDF417.

Each symbology has specific characteristics, such as the number of characters it can represent, error correction capabilities, and suitability for particular applications.

Choosing the Right Barcode

Selecting the appropriate barcode type and symbology is crucial for ensuring compatibility with systems and applications. Factors to consider include the industry, application requirements, data capacity, and scanning environment. Businesses should evaluate their specific needs and consult industry standards and regulations to make informed decisions when implementing barcode systems.

For retailers, the generally accepted barcodes on retail products are the UPC and EAN-13 barcodes. Ghanaian producers can choose any of the two; however, the UPC is priced higher compared to the EAN-13 by barcode retailers. QR codes can also be used, not as an alternative to the UPC/EAN-13, but as an additional barcode that enables details of the product, its origin and producer or other products by the producer.

A single product may have a QR and EAN-13 all together on its label. Whilst the EAN barcode will be use at the POS and for billing purposes (subject to editing by the individual stores), the QR will encode information by the producer. Information on QR may include producer details, batch number, manufacturing dates, website, contact details and any other such information as the producer may consider relevant. For regular QR, such encoded information cannot be changed on already printed tags, however, with dynamic QR; the information to be decoded can be edited even after printouts are made of the QR codes on the product labels through the backend link of the dynamic QR code.

Other industries may choose barcodes based on their requirements and industry standards but all such choices will revolve around the symbologies of Linear and 2D barcodes except for the publications and music industries where the ISBN/ISMN/ISSN are used appropriately.

Scanning and Reading Barcodes

Barcode scanners or readers are essential tools for capturing data from barcodes. Scanners use various technologies, such as laser scanning, linear imaging, or 2D imaging, to read barcodes accurately. Handheld scanners, fixed-mount scanners, and mobile devices equipped with built-in cameras can all serve as barcode readers. The scanned barcode data is then decoded and sent to a computer or system for further processing. A more elaborate write-up is in the hardware section of this book.

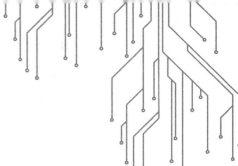

3.

Clarifying Common Misconceptions on Retail barcodes

1. Global Standard 1 (GS1) verses other barcode suppliers (Is it safe to buy retail barcodes from a resellers rather than from GS1?)

Not all retail barcodes sold on the internet are legitimate. Some barcode numbers may be illegal or may already be in use by another organization. This fear has resulted in the misconception that GS1 is the only medium to obtain legally registered barcode numbers. However, be assured that there are other barcode distributors whose barcodes are completely legit and accepted in as many countries and stores as possible.

The name Universal Product Code Council (UPCC) was changed to Universal Code Council (UCC) and then to GS1 in 2005 in a merger.

When GS1 merged with UCC (Uniform Code Council), GS1 had a class action lawsuit filed against it by the original UCC members relating to unnecessary membership fees. GS1 lost the case and had to forfeit control of the original barcodes and prefixes issued by the UCC, and license fees for these prefixes are no longer required for the old members whose memberships were reinforced without fees and charges by to GS1.

These numbers were bought by resellers and distributors and now been sold on an individual basis. They are new, unused, and still part of the GS1 system of which GS1 has full knowledge of. The Uniform Code Council (UCC) previously known as the UPCC is the original source from which all genuine barcodes originated and is now been managed and distributed by GS1 officially from February 2005 after battling and concluding with the 2002 lawsuit settlements.

One such trusted distributor with outlets in the majority of countries is the International Barcodes Network represented in Ghana as Barcodes Ghana (www.barcodesghana.com). Barcodes bought from this site are genuine, one-time payment, and orders are made and barcodes received completely online within minutes. A certificate is issued for each barcode or range of barcodes ordered to give assurance and proof of authenticity of the barcodes issued. All such barcodes can be verified from a global portal at www.ibnreg.org

Other worldwide distributors include mega barcodes, quality barcodes, world barcodes, and ISBN barcodes (for books).

It should be noted that, GS1 is a membership barcode distributor. This means, members must join the GS1 community, pay periodic renewal fees, and require a minimum number of products to register and get barcode allocation. Failure to pay annual renewal fees terminates your ownership of the barcodes meaning that barcodes from GS1 are still owned by GS1 and ownership is never transferred to businesses or producers who buy them.

Start-up businesses that require few barcodes to get into business may not have the initial muscle to meet all such requirements to have barcodes from GS1 hence the need for mini distributors who have their source of barcodes also from the same source as GS1.

2. The first three digits of a retail barcode indicate a product's country of origin.

My simple clarification to this is, it does not. This practice has become a myth overtime as it is no longer been adhered to.

A few of the supposed 3-digit country code allocations are below:
00 ~ 13 USA & CANADA 30 ~ 37 FRANCE 40 ~ 44 GERMANY 49 ~ JAPAN 50 ~ UK 57 ~ Denmark 64 ~ Finland 76 ~ Switzerland and Liechtenstein 471 ~ Taiwan 480 ~ Philippines 628 ~ Saudi-Arabien 629 ~ United Arab Emirates 690 ~ 695 China 740 ~ 745 Central America. Ghana specifically has 603.

To elaborate for you, I will repeat an excellent write-up by David Mikkelson, founder of snopes. David wrote "the 3-digit prefix code indicates which numbering organization has allocated the bank of numbers to the company. For example, a company may have its headquarters in South Africa. The EAN organization in South Africa has the code "600," but all the products of the company may be manufactured in England. The English-made products would still have the "600" prefix code. The prefix code is a way to have 70-plus EAN member organizations issuing numbers without having to worry about duplicate numbers". Again this idea is being championed strongly by GS1 through its outlets as opposed to other distributors like the International Barcodes Network (IBN).

This issue became intense in the wake of 2008 product scares involving melamine-tainted pet foods, lead-tainted toys, and melamine-tainted milk products, all originating in China. Consumers in the U.S. understandably became more apprehensive about the places of origin of the products they were purchasing.

Producers need not worry about this prefix concerns and should rather concentrate on ensuring they acquire barcodes within locations where major of their sales and administrative activities are undertaken. In Ghana for instance, products sold in major retail stores have barcodes starting with, 0770, 0951, 0670, 0721, 0630, 0130, 0634, 0413, 0743, 0781, 0966, and others. Hence, the myth or colonial practice of allocated codes is no longer active.

3. Retail Barcodes contain pricing information of the product

Again, a common misconception is that product barcodes directly encode the price of a product. In reality, barcodes typically represent a unique identifier for a product, such as its SKU (Stock Keeping Unit) or serial number. The actual pricing information is stored in the retailer's database or point-of-sale (POS) system, which is linked to the barcode. With EAN/UPC barcodes, the barcode serves as a medium through which the retail store can interact with the product by linking the barcode numbers or identifier with the system identity of the product thereby serving as a primary key for the product in the retailer's system in retrieving data on the product.

As a producer of the product, your responsibility is to ensure your product has a label with a genuine barcode on it. Each retailer will use their POS system to do pricing, description, and other such details as may be required for their business operations. Each retailer may give different prices; hence the idea that barcodes should contain product pricing is not right.

Due to this, major retailers of barcodes will not require any product information from the producer when orders are placed for barcodes but will require information about the business to whom or whose authority the barcodes are issued. Certificates of ownership for the range of barcodes issued are given in the name of the business with an indication of the range of barcodes issued. Hence, the important information in the ordering process is the business details.

4. If I scan my barcode on the internet, it should display details of my product, its origin and the company that produced it.

Many producers before buying a barcode ask the seller to ensure the barcodes are enlisted in search engines so that it can be seen anytime it is scanned on a search engine like Google. This is a unique feature that any producer can do for his range of products without the help of the barcode seller. This is called Google indexing and can be done through the Google console with your business registration ID.

This feature requires that you renew the indexing annually for the listing to continue to exist. Many barcode resellers avoid these feature since it add unnecessary cost to the pricing of the barcodes for starters and also make them commit to annual charges. It is absolutely fine to have barcodes without this feature since the retail store will work with them either way.

Some producers will use both an EAN and a static or regular QR code on their products to solve this matrix. The EAN will be for usage by the retail store whilst the QR code will contain generic details of the product and its origin. These QR can be scanned with a mobile phone with a QR application without internet requirements.

5. All retail barcodes are the same

Many people believe that all barcodes are identical and serve the same purpose. Contrary to this, there are multiple types of barcodes, each designed for specific applications and industries. Universal Product Codes (UPC) and European Article Numbers (EAN) are commonly used for retail products, while 2D codes are more versatile and can contain various types of data beyond product information (QR, Stacked), hence used in multiple industries.

ITF-14 or Carton Codes are created from EAN-13 and UPC-A barcodes. They are only used in production sites or warehouses on cartons containing a specific quantity of items and should not be used for any individual products that are for sale individually at the retail level.

Books and periodicals are all publications but require different barcodes all together including music and magazines.

Hence, depending on the industry, location and purpose of usage the appropriate barcode for use may differ.

6. Barcodes can be read by any scanner (Hardware related)

Though barcodes are generally designed to

be universally scannable, not all scanners can read every type of barcode. Different types of barcodes may require specific scanners or imaging technologies to be accurately decoded. For example, QR codes often require specialized smart phone apps or QR code readers to be scanned effectively. For retail barcodes, only retailers who have encoded the product into their system and link the barcode will have a successful scan. For instance, a UPC barcode on a product not yet accepted by Amazon will not display any information when scanned by their system. To use a local example in Ghana, a product not yet accepted by Melcom shopping mall will not display any product information when scanned but may display information if already on the shelves of Accra mall and vice versa. Hence, the importance of the encoding technology discussed earlier comes to full effect in deciding which scanners to use.

7. Barcodes are only used for retail purposes

While retail applications are prevalent, barcodes usages have expanded across various industries. Barcodes are employed in healthcare for patient identification, medication tracking, in logistics for inventory management and tracking shipments, in libraries for cataloguing books, and in manufacturing for tracking components and streamlining production processes.

A note of caution however is that, there exist different barcode symbologies for different purposes and some have legislative requirements to use a particular type. Hence, practitioners may have to check with the industry requirements in making a choice.

8. I can use one barcode for all my retail products

Many start-up business owners consider ordering a single barcode for all their catalogues of products. Products differ in brands, Sizes, Colours, and Flavours (BSCF).

Each of these four attributes when used to differentiate a product should be enough a reason to order a unique barcode for that product range. The purpose of barcoding is defeated if a single barcode is used on multiple products or a similar product with different variant. Retail stores will automatically reject such products. Below provides a guide in determining how many barcodes to order.

		Brand	Size	Colour	Flavour	Total barcodes to Order
Product A	Ideal Milk	1 (Nestle)	1 (330ml)	1 (regular)	1 (original)	1 barcode to order (1*1*1 = 1)
Product B	Mentos Gum	1 (Mentos)	2 (11.45g, 20g)	1 (white)	1	2 barcodes to order. (1*2*1 = 2)

- *Please note to multiply through all the boxes.*

In conclusion, Understanding these misconceptions about barcodes can help businesses and individuals make informed decisions when implementing barcode systems.

4.

Barcodes for the Novice Producer and How it Can Benefit Them

Start-up businesses must appreciate the important role product barcodes play in scaling product sales, protecting brands and guiding businesses into the future in general. Barcodes provide numerous benefits that can help streamline operations, enhance product visibility, and facilitate growth for novice producers. We will explore why obtaining barcodes for products is a wise decision and how it can contribute to their success.

Streamlined Inventory Management Process
- For novice producers, efficient inventory management is crucial. Barcodes simplify inventory tracking by providing a standardized and automated system for product identification. By assigning unique barcodes to each product, producers can easily track stock levels, monitor product movement, and automate inventory control processes. This streamlined operation,

reduce manual errors, and ensures accurate stock counts, helping producers maintain optimal inventory levels and avoid stock outs or overstocking.

- **Enhanced Product Visibility**
The use of barcodes plays a significant role in increasing product visibility and marketability. Many retailers and online marketplaces require products to have barcodes for easy and efficient scanning at the point of sale. By obtaining product barcodes, producers can expand their distribution channels and reach a wider audience through retail partnerships, online platforms, and e-commerce marketplaces. Barcodes enable products to be easily scanned and tracked, making them more appealing to retailers and enhancing their market presence.

- **Efficient Order Fulfilment**
Efficient order fulfilment is essential for producers to meet customer expectations and build a positive reputation. Barcodes simplify the order fulfilment process by enabling accurate order processing. When barcodes are scanned during the picking and packing stages, producers can ensure the correct products are selected, reducing the risk of errors and customer dissatisfaction. Barcode-based order fulfilment improves accuracy, speeds up processing times,

and enhances overall customer satisfaction.

* **Accurate tracking of Sales and Finances**
  For emerging producers, keeping track of sales and financial data is vital for business growth and decision-making. Barcodes provide a reliable basis for accurately capturing sales transactions. By scanning barcodes, producers can automatically record sales data, track product performance, and analyze sales trends. This information enables better inventory management, pricing strategies, and forecasting. This empowers novice producers to make data-driven decisions and optimize their business operations for tax, regulatory and funding compliance.

Counterfeit Prevention

Protecting products from counterfeiting is a concern for many a producer. Barcodes can serve as powerful tools in counterfeit prevention. Do not limit your scope to supermarket products. The concept is on all produced items; hence all categories of barcodes are in focus.

Electronic products have inbuilt serial numbers that are unique to each device and can be entirely traced to its origin, time of production and details of production notes. These serial numbers are usually different from the product model numbers which are the same for each category of items. For instance, 50pcs of Samsung 32'' digital satellite TV can be produced on Monday. All of these quantities will have the same model but individual serial numbers will be unique to each TV.

An outlier is unable to fit into any of the range of serial numbers issued hence easily detected. Many retail stores use this feature to cut or reduce cost on warranty schemes (after sales support) for devices not sold by their stores but are being brought for repairs to enjoy warranty benefits. Once the serials of all the units sold in the store are maintained, any unrelated product is easily identified. In practice, many retail and departmental stores designate staffs in charge of registering and recording the serials of products sold. This is then linked to the customer data in their system for future referencing. This protection against counterfeiting helps build brand credibility, maintain customer trust, and safeguard the reputation of novice producers as they grow and build their businesses.

Scaling and Expansion Opportunities
As producers aim for growth and expansion, barcodes pave the way for scalability. Barcodes enable producers to seamlessly integrate with supply chain partners, retailers, and e-commerce platforms. By complying with industry standards of obtaining barcodes, producers position themselves

for growth, enhance operational efficiency, and establish credibility within their respective industries. Barcodes also facilitate the ability to enter new markets, expand distribution networks, and adapt to evolving customer demands.

Producers of products, enjoy much better returns if the retailers are able to maximize their sales through the efficient use of barcodes that facilitate their processes. The supplier gets paid on time through an easy reconciliation process aided by the product barcodes. Orders are placed for specific items to the supplier by referencing the barcodes of the product and their stock-keeping-units (SKUs)

In essence, barcodes serve the needs of both the producers and the sellers. As a condition for acceptance of products into a retail store, all retailers will require a barcode on the product.

In conclusion, product barcodes come in various forms and play vital roles in the modern business landscape. They streamline inventory management, expedite transactions, provide accurate product information, and enhance customer service. By leveraging the power of barcodes, businesses can operate more efficiently, make data-driven decisions, and ultimately thrive in the competitive marketplace.

5.

The Role of Barcodes in Supply Chain Management

This chapter focuses on the critical role that all barcodes play in supply chain management. It highlights how barcodes enable efficient tracking of products from manufacturing to distribution and retail. The chapter explores barcode-based inventory management systems, discussing how businesses can optimize stock levels, streamline order fulfilment, and improve overall supply chain visibility. It also delves into the use of barcodes for traceability, allowing businesses to quickly identify and address issues related to product recalls or quality control.

Barcode-Driven Inventory Management
Barcodes have transformed inventory management by providing accurate and real-time visibility into stock levels. Through the use of barcode technology, businesses can track the movement of products,

monitor stock quantities, and automate reorder processes. Barcode-based inventory management systems ensure that businesses maintain optimal inventory levels, minimize stock-outs, and reduce the carrying costs associated with excess inventory. With the ability to scan barcodes, inventory personnel can easily update stock records, trigger alerts for replenishment, and perform cycle counting efficiently. This level of accuracy and automation improves inventory accuracy, reduces manual errors, and streamlines the overall inventory control process.

Streamlining Logistics and Distribution

Barcodes are invaluable in streamlining logistics and distribution operations. When products are labelled with barcodes, they can be scanned at various points along the supply chain, providing a clear audit trail and enhancing visibility. Barcode scanning enables efficient tracking of shipments, ensuring that products reach their intended destinations promptly. In warehouses and distribution centres, barcode scanning optimizes the process of picking, packing, and shipping. Warehouse personnel can scan barcodes to accurately identify and locate products, minimizing errors and expediting order fulfilment. This result in faster turnaround times, reduced labour costs, and improved customer satisfaction.

Product Traceability and Compliance

Barcodes play a vital role in ensuring product traceability and compliance within the supply chain. By encoding unique identifiers in barcodes, businesses can track and trace products throughout their journey from manufacturer to consumer. This capability is especially critical in industries such as food, pharmaceuticals, and electronics, where product safety, quality, and regulatory compliance are of utmost importance.

In the event of a product recall on quality issue, barcodes enable businesses to quickly and accurately identify affected products and take necessary actions to protect consumers. Barcode-based traceability systems provide the necessary data to locate specific batches, identify suppliers, and communicate with stakeholders effectively. This is an emphasis on the concept of serialization.

Improved Data Accuracy and Analytics

One of the significant advantages of barcodes in supply chain management is the ability to capture data accurately and consistently. Barcode scanning eliminates manual data entry errors, ensuring that the information captured is reliable and up to date. This accuracy extends to areas such as product identification, serial numbers, lot numbers, and expiration dates, which are vital for quality control and regulatory compliance.

The data collected through barcode scanning provides businesses with valuable insights to data analytics and decision-making. By analyzing barcode data, businesses can identify trends, optimize inventory levels, forecast demand, and make informed strategic decisions that improve supply chain efficiency.

Enhancing Efficiency at the Point of Sale (POS)
- **Streamlining the Checkout Process**
  Barcode scanning has revolutionized the checkout process, making it faster, more efficient, and less prone to errors. With barcodes on retail products, cashiers can simply scan products, automatically retrieving the product information and pricing from the database. This eliminates the need for manual entry or searching, memorising prices, speeding up the transaction process and reducing the time customers spend at the checkout counter. Retailers rely on this to monitor their performance, improve efficiency and create competitive advantage in serving the customer.

- **Accuracy in Pricing and Product Identification**
  Barcodes ensure accurate pricing at the point of sale. By scanning the barcode, the POS system

retrieves the product's pricing information from the database, eliminating the risk of human error or pricing inconsistencies. Customers can have confidence that they are being charged the correct amount for their purchases, enhancing trust and customer satisfaction.

Additionally, barcodes provide reliable product identification. Each barcode is unique to a specific product, allowing the POS system to retrieve accurate and detailed information about the product, such as its description, attributes, and any applicable discounts or promotions. This information helps both the cashier and the customer ensure that the correct product is being purchased.

- **Efficient Integration with Inventory Management**
  Barcodes play a vital role in integrating the point of sale with inventory management systems. When a barcode is scanned at the checkout counter, the inventory management system is immediately updated, reflecting the reduction in stock levels. This real-time inventory visibility enables businesses to monitor stock levels accurately, automate reordering processes, and avoid stock-outs or overstocking.

- **Improved Customer Experience**
  Barcode scanning technology significantly enhances the customer experience at the point of sale. The speed and accuracy of barcode scanning minimize wait times and reduce frustration for customers. The checkout process becomes seamless and efficient, improving customer satisfaction and building positive brand impressions.

  Barcode scanning also allows for smooth and hassle-free returns and exchanges. By scanning the barcode on the receipt or the product itself or using the receipt numbers, businesses can quickly identify the original purchase, verify its authenticity, and process the return or exchange efficiently. This streamlines the return process for both customers and businesses, fostering customer loyalty and satisfaction.

- **Advancements in POS Technology**
  The integration of barcode scanning technology has spurred advancements in POS technology. Traditional barcode scanners have evolved into more compact and versatile devices, including handheld scanners and built-in scanner modules in tablets and smart-phones. These advancements have allowed businesses to offer flexible checkout options, such as mobile

POS systems or self-checkout kiosks, further enhancing the efficiency of the checkout process. There are in-store price verification points for customers. This verification points are simply scannable devices mounted at various locations within the store where customers can confirm prices without having to visit the cashier or the billing counter.

Moreover, barcode scanning technology has paved the way for contactless payment systems, such as mobile wallets and payment apps. With the scan of a barcode or QR code, customers can complete transactions securely and conveniently using their smartphones. This enables businesses to provide a seamless and modern payment experience, aligning with evolving customer preferences.

6.

Book Barcodes & Identifiers Including Magazines, Periodicals & Music – ISBN/ISSN/ISMN

Introduction

Writing a book is a patient process and should have some flexibility on the timelines but surprisingly authors mostly want to rush through the publication process. The publication stage should equally be a well planned process because a mistake at this stage can cost enormous amount of resource wastages. As such, one critical item in any publication checklist should be to get the right barcode.

The writer must first be clear minded on the write-up category. Publications are either qualified for ISBN, ISSN or ISMN. Retail or product barcodes like EAN, UPC, ITF numbers are not to be used in these cases. The symbology of EAN or UPC may be used but not the numbers.

For instance, an ISBN maybe issued and a EAN image can be generated with the number for a book. This is entirely ok but differs from using an EAN as an ISBN which is also a 13-digit number.

EAN images can be the barcode format of the ISBN assigned to books when the number is generated from a regulated source.

The bone of contention here is the source of the numbers been used to form the symbol or image. If the ISB numbers are issued correctly, then your image or symbology can be that of an EAN but you cannot use an EA number to represent an ISB number. The example of image and number contention applies to ISBN, ISSN and ISMN.

QR codes may play a different role on the book cover but not as a standard identifier. Some authors use QR to direct readers to their book list or website or sell other products.

The ISBN – International Standard Book Number
The ISBN (International Standard Book Number) is intended for monographic publications. This is text that stands on its own as a product, whether printed, audio or electronic. ISBNs are never assigned to categories like music, performances or images, such as art prints or photographs. ISBNs are not

assigned to magazines, academic journals or other periodicals. However, if a single issue of a periodical is being sold as a book, then that issue alone may be assigned an ISBN and not an ISSN or any other barcode.

ISBNs up till December 2006 were 10 digits. The new ranges beginning 2007 are all 13 digits and are either initiated with 978 or 979. These 13-digit long numbers represents five unique combinations of numbers including the prefix, Registration group element, Registrant element, Publication element, and the Check digit.

It is dangerous to fabricate an ISBN because any such fabrication will violate all the five standard categories mentioned above and the ideal purpose for using the ISBN as an identifier will have failed.

The ISSN - International Standard Serial Numbers
The ISSN (the International Standard Serial Numbers) are 8 digit numbers (e.g. 1234-567x) allocated to all periodical publications such as magazines or journals. An ISSN consists of 8- digits, specifically two groups of four set of digits, except for the last digit, which can be an X, the rest are numbers. Its proper reference is for the two groups of four digits to be separated by a hyphen and preceded by the letters ISSN – (ISSN 1234 – 567X).

The Music Barcode – ISMN

The International Standard Music Number (ISMN) is a unique identifier for notated music (scores, parts, vocal scores, choral octavos, miniature scores, pop folios, etc.) whether published in print, online, or in other media. Each edition or version of a musical work is assigned a separate ISMN. Each separately available constituent part of a publication is assigned its own ISMN.

The ISMN is useful in music publishing, the music trade, and music libraries. It is used for inventory, ordering, billing, rights assessment, information retrieval, and library circulation. The ISMN serves as a unique identifier for a monographic publication, from manuscript stage through editorial and manufacturing processes until the work is finished. ISMN are comprised of 13 digits divided into four elements or parts, Prefix element (always 979-0, denoting music), Publisher element (variable in length), Item element (variable in length), Check digit (validating the number).

Prolific publishers receive an identifier of three or four digits; smaller publishers receive identifiers of five, six, or seven digits.

Prior to January 1, 2008, ISMN consisted of ten digits, divided into four elements. These older ISMN are often encountered on earlier music publications and function just as the currently used 13-digit numbers.

Where to Get ISBN/ISSN/ISMN

Each country has a designated institution in charge of issuing genuine barcodes for all the above publications.

In Ghana, the only institution with the mandate of issuing these numbers is the George Padmore Research Library located within the Ministries in Accra. The numbers can be ordered online via their portal at www.isbn.library.gov.gh.

Other countries can check the following website for country specific institutions:- *www.isbn-international.org*

Unlike retail barcodes, ISBN, ISSN and ISMN are not retailed by other distributors. Distributors may regenerate barcode images with the numbers issued by the designated authorities but not to issue the actual numbers.

To verify whether a publication number is genuine or fake, it has to be referenced to the only institution mandated to issue those numbers for authentication. It is hoped that, this section of the book will provide enough guide to authors, publishers and producers of musicals.

7.

Barcode-Based Loyalty Programs

The Power of Barcode-Based Loyalty Programs

Barcode-based loyalty programs offer businesses a powerful way to incentivize and reward customers for their repeat business. Barcodes provide a platform where businesses provide customers with unique barcode-based loyalty cards or mobile apps which customers use when they make transactions. In one hand, the customer gets value for using the program in the form of discounts, coupons, and promotion alerts. On the other hand, businesses can track and capture customer data, allowing for personalized offers, tailored promotions, and enhanced customer experiences.

In crafting these schemes, businesses should envisage the possibility of misuse either by the customer or employees of the business. Any such misuse will influence the data been used for analysing customer purchase history and preferences. A Reward scheme for loyalty has to be on genuine data of actual purchase history by the individual customer. This ensures the achievement of the objective for which the program has been initiated.

For both the business and its clientele, the benefits of these schemes are enormous and include the briefs below.

Capturing Customer Data and Behaviour

Barcode evolution has enable businesses to capture valuable customer data and behaviour through loyalty programs. Each time customers scans a loyalty cards or apps at the point of sale, their purchases are linked to their unique barcode. This data provides insights into customer preferences, purchase history, and spending patterns, enabling businesses to create targeted marketing campaigns and personalized offers based on individual customer profiles. Whilst the business a database of customers to relate with, the customer gets free updates on incentive schemes which the ordinary customer will not be easily get.

With the issue of customer data however, it is important to note that, there are country specific regulations that apply in using such data especially for commercial purposes. Businesses should ensure compliance with such regulations to avoid customer privacy issues.

Tailored Marketing and Personalized Offers

With barcode-based loyalty programs, businesses can deliver personalized marketing initiatives to customers. By leveraging the captured customer data, businesses can segment customers into specific target groups and create tailored marketing campaigns. This personalization allows businesses to offer relevant promotions, discounts, and rewards based on customers' past purchases, preferences, and shopping habits.

For instance, a supermarket may offer exclusive discounts on products that customers frequently purchase or provide personalized recommendations based on their shopping history. These targeted offers enhance customer engagement, increase the likelihood of repeat purchases, and foster a sense of appreciation and loyalty towards the brand.

Enhancing the Customer Experience

Barcode-based loyalty programs also contribute to an enhanced customer experience. With loyalty cards or mobile apps featuring barcodes, customers can enjoy loyalty programs without the need for physical membership cards or cumbersome paperwork. The convenience and ease of scanning the barcode at the point of sale provide a seamless and frictionless experience for customers, encouraging participation and engagement.

Furthermore, barcode-based loyalty programs allow businesses to offer additional benefits and perks to loyal customers. These benefits can include priority access to new products or services, special events, personalized recommendations, or even VIP treatment. Such exclusive rewards create a sense of exclusivity and strengthen the bond between the customer and the brand.

Tracking and Evaluating Program Effectiveness

Barcode-based loyalty programs provide businesses with the ability to track and evaluate the effectiveness of their loyalty initiatives. By analyzing barcode data and tracking customer participation, businesses can measure the impact of loyalty programs on customer retention, average transaction value, and overall profitability. This data-driven evaluation allows businesses to refine and optimize their loyalty strategies for better results.

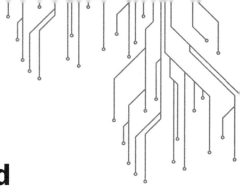

8.

Barcodes and E-commerce

Introduction

In the fast-paced world of e-commerce, efficiency and accuracy are paramount. Consumers expect speedy deliveries, seamless returns, and transparent inventory updates. Barcodes, those seemingly simple black and white stripes, hold the key to unlocking these desired qualities. This chapter delves into the world of barcodes and e-commerce, exploring their vital role in optimizing your business operations and enhancing customer experience.

Barcode Types for E-commerce

While the familiar Universal Product Code (UPC) is widely used, various barcode types cater to specific e-commerce needs:

- GS1-128 (UCC-128): Provides greater data capacity for product descriptions, weights, and serial numbers.

- EAN-13/UPC-A: Standard product identification for retail goods.
- QR Codes: Popular for linking to product pages, promotions, or mobile apps.
- Data Matrix: Smaller and complex, often used for smaller items or tracking.

Benefits of Barcodes in E-commerce

- **Accurate Product Identification and Data Capture**

  Barcodes serve as a reliable and efficient method for identifying products in the e-commerce environment. Each product is labelled with a unique barcode that can be scanned or entered manually into e-commerce systems. This accurate product identification eliminates the risk of errors in product selection, ensuring that customers receive the exact items ordered.

  Barcode scanning technology allows e-commerce businesses to capture and integrate product data seamlessly. By scanning barcodes during the inventory intake process, businesses can automatically populate product information, including descriptions, specifications, pricing, and images, into their e-commerce platforms. This streamlined data capture process ensures that accurate and up-to-date product information is readily available to customers.

- **Streamlined Order Fulfilment and Shipping**
  Barcodes play a crucial role in streamlining the order fulfilment process in e-commerce operations. When an order is received, barcode scanning technology enables warehouse personnel to locate and pick the correct products quickly and accurately. By scanning barcodes on products and packaging, businesses can validate order accuracy and reduce errors in fulfilment.

  Barcode scanning also facilitates efficient shipping and tracking. When packages are prepared for shipment, barcodes can be scanned to generate shipping labels and capture tracking information. This enables customers to track their orders in real-time, providing transparency and enhancing the overall customer experience.

- **Boosting Warehouse Efficiency**
  Warehouses are the beating heart of e-commerce, and barcodes can inject a powerful dose of efficiency into their operations. With scanning technology, picking and sorting become significantly faster and more accurate. Imagine scanning a barcode instead of manually searching for items, reducing picking time and minimizing errors. Furthermore, barcodes streamline put-away processes; ensuring

products are directed to the correct locations effortlessly. Cycle counts become a breeze, eliminating the need for tedious physical counts and discrepancies. This translates to faster order fulfilment, reduced labour costs, and increased overall warehouse throughput. Barcodes aren't just about tracking items; they're about optimizing the flow of your entire warehouse operation, ultimately delivering products to your customers quicker and more efficiently.

- **Seamless Integration with E-commerce Platforms**
  Barcodes seamlessly integrate with e-commerce platforms, ensuring efficient data exchange and smooth operations. E-commerce systems can be configured to recognize and process barcode data, automating tasks such as inventory updates, order management, and fulfilment tracking. This integration eliminates manual data entry, reduces errors, and accelerates order processing.

Barcode scanning technology allows e-commerce businesses to offer diverse fulfilment options, such as ship-from-store or click-and-collect. By scanning barcodes during the order fulfilment process, businesses can determine the optimal location for product fulfilment, whether it's a centralized warehouse or a nearby retail store. This flexibility in fulfilment options enables businesses to provide faster delivery, reduce shipping costs, and enhance customer convenience.

- **Returns and Exchanges Made Efficient**
  Barcodes simplify the process of returns and exchanges in the e-commerce environment. When customers need to return or exchange a product, barcode scanning enables businesses to quickly and accurately identify the original purchase, validate its condition, and process the return or exchange efficiently. Barcode-based returns streamline the workflow, reducing processing time and improving customer satisfaction.

Barcode scanning also helps businesses track and manage returned products. By scanning barcodes on returned items, businesses can update inventory records, identify patterns of returns, and analyze reasons for returns. This data allows businesses to identify opportunities for product improvements, customer service enhancements, and overall operational optimizations.

- **Inventory Management Transformed**
  Gone are the days of manual counts and spreadsheets leading to stock-outs and overstocking. Barcodes act as the magic key to unlocking real-time inventory visibility. With a simple scan, you can track product movement across warehouses, fulfilment centres, and even individual shelves. The accuracy eliminates discrepancies, prevents costly errors, and allows for optimized ordering and resource allocation. Imagine instantly identifying low stock levels and triggering automatic replenishment or pinpointing misplaced items with ease. Barcodes not only save time and money but also ensure your customers receive their orders promptly and without hassle.

Conclusion

Barcodes are not just relics of the brick-and-mortar era; they are powerful tools for maximizing efficiency and accuracy in the dynamic world of e-commerce. By embracing barcoding technology, businesses can streamline operations, enhance customer experience, and gain a competitive edge in the digital marketplace.

Remember, barcodes are a foundational technology, but their true value lies in how they are integrated into your overall e-commerce ecosystem. With the right planning and implementation, barcodes can unlock a world of possibilities for your business growth.

9.

Decoding the Scan

Barcode Scanning Technology and Hardware

Barcodes have revolutionized the supply chain, but capturing their encoded information requires specialized tools. This section delves into the fascinating world of barcode scanning technology and the diverse hardware that unlocks the data trapped within those lines. Buckle up, retail adventurers, as we embark on a journey through lasers, cameras, and the unsung heroes of information capture.

Types of Barcode Scanners

1. **Laser Scanners:** Laser scanners are one of the most common types of barcode scanners. They use a laser beam to illuminate and read the barcodes by detecting the reflection of light from the barcode's black and white spaces. The reflected light creates a pattern, interpreted by a sensor and translated into data. Laser scanners

are known for their accuracy and ability to read barcodes from a distance.

2. **Linear Imaging Scanners (charged coupled device - CCD):** Linear imaging scanners, also known as linear imagers or CCD scanners, use a charged coupled device (CCD) to capture barcode data. They work by using an array of light-sensitive diodes that captures the barcode image and then decoding it using image processing techniques. Linear imagers are often more durable and cost-effective than laser scanners.

3. **2D Imaging Scanners (Image Scanners):** 2D imaging scanners utilize image capture technology to read both linear and two-dimensional barcodes. They use a combination of cameras and image processing algorithms to capture and decode barcode data. 2D imagers are versatile and can read barcodes from various angles, making them suitable for reading QR codes and other complex symbologies.

4. **Omnidirectional Scanners:** Omnidirectional scanners use multiple scanning lines to read barcodes from any direction, eliminating the need for precise alignment. They are commonly used in high-volume retail environments where

fast and efficient scanning is required.

Each technology has its advantages and limitations. Laser scanners are fast and affordable, but struggle with curved surfaces and poor-quality codes. CCD scanners handle damaged codes well but lack speed. Imager scanners are versatile but may be pricier. Choosing the right one depends on your specific needs.

Barcode Scanning Hardware

1. **Handheld Scanners:** Handheld scanners are portable devices that are held by an operator and manually passed over the barcode to capture the data. They come in various form factors, including corded and cordless options. Handheld scanners provide flexibility and ease of use, making them suitable for a wide range of applications.

2. **Fixed-Mount Scanners:** Fixed-mount scanners are designed to be mounted or installed in a fixed position, such as on a conveyor belt or at a workstation. They are commonly used in automated systems where barcodes need to be scanned quickly and accurately without manual intervention.

3. **Mobile Scanning Devices:** Mobile scanning devices, such as smartphones and tablets equipped with built-in cameras, can also function as barcode scanners. With the help of barcode scanning apps, these devices can capture barcode data and integrate it with various applications or systems. Mobile scanning devices provide mobility and convenience, making them suitable for inventory management, retail, and field service applications.

4. **Rugged Scanners:** Built for harsh conditions like warehouses or construction sites, these scanners can withstand drops, dust, and moisture. Some even offer extended reading ranges for scanning pallets or stacked items.

5. **Ring Scanners:** Worn on the finger, these lightweight options enable hands-free scanning while leaving the wearer's hands free for other tasks. Perfect for picking and packing applications.

6. **Wearable Scanners:** Mounted on arms or glasses, these futuristic options offer hands-free and heads-up scanning, maximizing worker productivity in tasks like order fulfilment or quality control.

In conclusion on this, it is important to state that the "best" scanner depends on your specific needs and budget. Consider factors like scanning volume, barcode types, environment, and user comfort.

Advancements in Barcode Scanning Technology

1. **Wireless Connectivity:** Modern barcode scanners often incorporate wireless connectivity options, such as Bluetooth or Wi-Fi, enabling seamless integration with various devices and systems. Wireless scanners provide freedom of movement, increased flexibility, and enhanced convenience.

2. **Image-Based Decoding:** Barcode scanning technology has advanced to include image-based decoding algorithms that can read damaged or poorly printed barcodes more accurately. These algorithms utilize image processing techniques to enhance image quality and improve the decoding success rate.

3. **Data Capture and Integration:** Barcode scanning technology has evolved to facilitate the capture and integration of barcode data into various systems and applications. Scanners can connect directly to computers, point-of-sale systems, or mobile devices, enabling real-time data transfer and integration.

4. **Durability and Ruggedness:** Barcode scanners designed for industrial or harsh environments often feature rugged construction, with resistance to drops, spills, and dust. These durable scanners ensure reliable performance even in demanding conditions.

Beyond the Beep: Emerging Trends in Scanner Technology and their Impact on Retail

The unassuming barcode scanner, once a simple tool for reading prices, is undergoing a metamorphosis. Fuelled by advancements in technology, new trends are emerging, poised to reshape the retail landscape. A few of the innovations and their potential impact on the retail industry are explored below.

- **Smart Scanners and the Rise of Data**
  Scanners are no longer just data readers; they're becoming data collectors. Integration with Artificial Intelligence (AI) allows them to extract additional information, like product origin, expiration dates, or even customer preferences. Imagine a scanner recognizing a specific brand of wine and suggesting food pairings on the spot, or automatically adding items to a loyalty program. This enriched data empowers retailers to personalize the shopping experience, optimize inventory management, and gain deeper insights into customer behaviour.

- **Sensor Fusion for Enhanced Functionality**
Modern scanners are shedding their single-purpose nature, incorporating multiple sensors like cameras, depth sensors, and even LiDAR (Light Detection and Ranging). This sensor fusion enables functionalities beyond barcode reading. Visualize a scanner identifying damaged goods on shelves, detecting counterfeit products, or even tracking inventory in real-time through Radio Frequency Identification (RFID) tags. This versatility promises increased efficiency, improved loss prevention, and automated stock management.

- **The Rise of Biometric Authentication**
Biometric scanners, previously confined to high-security areas, are finding their way into retail. Picture scanning your fingerprint or iris to pay for groceries or unlock personalized offers. This technology promises faster and more secure checkout experiences, potentially eliminating the need for physical cards and passwords. However, concerns around data privacy and security need to be addressed before widespread adoption.

- **The Blurring Lines Between Physical and Digital**
The integration of Augmented Reality (AR) with scanners is creating immersive shopping

experiences. Imagine scanning a product and seeing virtual models showcasing different colours or sizes, or accessing product information and reviews overlaid on the actual item. This technology can increase engagement, improve product understanding, and potentially drive sales.

- **The Collaborative Scanner Ecosystem**
Scanners are no longer standalone devices; they're becoming part of a connected ecosystem. Integration with Internet of Things (IoT) platforms allows real-time data sharing and collaboration between different devices. Imagine a scanner notifying a nearby robot to restock a depleted shelf or triggering automated price adjustments based on demand. This interconnectedness promises streamlined operations, optimized logistics, and dynamic pricing strategies.

Impact on the Retail Industry

These emerging trends hold immense potential for the retail industry:

- **Enhanced Customer Experience:** Personalized offers, faster checkouts, and interactive product information can lead to happier and more engaged customers.
- **Improved Operational Efficiency:** Automated tasks, real-time data insights, and optimized

inventory management can significantly reduce costs and boost efficiency.

- **Data-Driven Decision Making:** Richer data collection can fuel better inventory planning, targeted marketing campaigns, and improved pricing strategies.
- **Loss Prevention and Security:** Advanced sensors and authentication methods can help combat theft and counterfeit products, improving security and reducing losses.

However, with such emergence, below challenges are envisaged to remain until wider implementation across major retail outlets and destinations around the globe. This is a common challenge with technological innovations.

- **Cost and Implementation:** New technologies come with higher costs and require infrastructure upgrades, posing a hurdle for smaller retailers.
- **Data Privacy and Security:** Biometric authentication and data collection raise concerns that need to be addressed through robust security measures and clear data privacy policies.
- **Consumer Adoption:** Some technologies might face resistance from consumers who value traditional shopping experiences or have privacy concerns.

The future of retail scanning is bright, brimming with possibilities. As these trends mature and become more accessible, we can expect a retail landscape transformed by intelligent, connected, and data-driven scanners.

However, navigating the challenges and ensuring responsible implementation will be crucial to unlocking the full potential of this technological revolution. By embracing these innovations thoughtfully, retailers can create a more efficient, engaging, and personalized shopping experience for customers, ultimately securing their place in the ever-evolving retail ecosystem.

Barcode scanning technology and hardware play a vital role in capturing and decoding barcode data accurately and efficiently. With various types of scanners available, businesses can select the most suitable option based on their specific requirements and industry needs. Advancements in barcode scanning technology, including wireless connectivity, image-based decoding, and seamless integration, have further enhanced the capabilities and convenience of barcode scanners.

Chapter Case Study
AutoZone Speeds Up Parts Delivery with Rugged Mobile Scanners

AutoZone, a leading retailer of auto parts, faced a challenge: their manual inventory management system was slow and error-prone, leading to delays in parts delivery and frustrated customers. To address this, they implemented a new solution focused on mobile barcode scanning technology.

Hardware Components

- **Rugged Mobile Computers:** AutoZone equipped employees with Zebra TC52x mobile computers. These rugged devices featured:
- **Integrated laser scanner:** For fast and accurate reading of barcodes on various parts, even in low-light conditions.
- **Large touch screen display:** For easy access to inventory information and order processing.
- **Durable design:** Withstands drops, dust, and moisture, ideal for the warehouse environment.
- **Wireless connectivity:** Enables real-time data transmission and communication with back-end systems.

Benefits

- **Increased Speed and Efficiency:** Mobile scanners enabled employees to scan parts directly on shelves and in customer vehicles, eliminating the need for manual data entry and saving valuable time.

- **Improved Accuracy:** Real-time scanning reduced errors associated with manual data entry, ensuring accurate inventory levels and order fulfilment.
- **Enhanced Customer Service:** Faster processing allowed employees to spend more time assisting customers, providing a better overall experience.
- **Optimized Inventory Management:** Real-time data insights helped AutoZone optimize stock levels, reduce stock outs, and improve space utilization.

Key Hardware Considerations

- **Choosing the right scanner:** AutoZone opted for laser scanners for their speed and reliability in reading various barcodes. Imager scanners might be suitable for damaged codes or 2D codes.
- **Ruggedness:** The warehouse environment demanded robust devices like the TC52x, but other businesses might opt for lighter scanners depending on their needs.
- **Connectivity:** Wireless connectivity was crucial for real-time data transmission and integration with existing systems.

Impact

The implementation of mobile barcode scanning technology led to:

- 25% reduction in order processing time
- 99.5% inventory accuracy
- Increased customer satisfaction

Conclusion

This case study demonstrates how choosing the right hardware components, like rugged mobile computers with integrated scanners, and how it can significantly impact a retail business's efficiency, accuracy, and customer service. By carefully considering the specific needs of your environment and tasks, you can select the optimal hardware to optimize your barcode scanning solution and unlock its full potential.

10.

Beyond Retail: Applications of Barcodes in Other Industries

In this chapter, we will explore the diverse applications of barcodes beyond the retail industry. While barcodes are commonly associated with product identification and sale transactions, their benefits extend to various other sectors. We will examine how barcodes are utilized in industries such as healthcare, manufacturing, transportation, libraries, and more. These applications highlight the versatility and value of barcodes in different contexts. The barcodes mentioned here are not limited to only retail barcodes like the EAN, UPC, ITF but extends to other 2D barcodes like the QR, Data Matrix, Stacked and ISBN/ISSN/ISMN depending on the industry and purpose of the requirements for the barcode.

1. Healthcare

Barcodes have revolutionized healthcare operations, improving patient safety, medication tracking, and inventory management. In hospitals and clinics, barcodes are used to identify patients, ensuring accurate administration of medications and treatments. Medication barcodes enable healthcare professionals to verify the correct medication, dosage, and patient information, reducing medication errors.

The barcoding systems within the healthcare sector have gone through a lot of arguments in relation to which acceptable system to use. To spare you of the unnecessary details, below is quoted from the Medical Device & Diagnostic Industry Magazine (MDDI) in a comprehensive write-up by Walter W. Mosher on the journey of the medical association in barcoding.

"Thus, at the present time, it is correct to use either the UCC/EAN or HIBCC standard. These standards will be accepted worldwide based on the agreement between the UCC/EAN and the European HIBCC, and will also be satisfactory for the DOD and many other government agencies, such as California's Medi-Cal".

Hence it is safe to sell UCC/EAN/UPC barcodes for medications that are retailed to customers. The UPN will be ideal for producers in the US who have the identification numbers.

2. Manufacturing

Barcodes are instrumental in streamlining manufacturing processes, enabling efficient tracking of raw materials, work-in-progress items, and finished goods. By labelling components and products with barcodes, manufacturers can easily identify and trace items throughout the production cycle. Barcode scanning automates data capture, improving inventory accuracy, reducing manual errors, and enhancing overall supply chain visibility. Many manufacturing setups have developed or acquired comprehensive off the shelve ERP packaged that help with the labelling of manufacturing components and tracking of assets for automated fault reports and maintenance workflows.

3. Construction and Engineering
- **Material tracking:** Track building materials from purchase to installation using barcodes, optimizing inventory control and reducing waste.
- **Equipment maintenance:** Implement barcode-based maintenance schedules and inspections for preventive maintenance and extended

equipment life.

- **As-built drawings:** Overlay barcodes on as-built drawings to link physical components with digital information for efficient maintenance and future reference.

4. Transportation and Logistics

In the transportation and logistics industry, barcodes play a vital role in tracking shipments, improving accuracy, and optimizing operations. Barcodes are used on shipping labels and packaging to capture essential information, such as origin, destination, and tracking numbers. Barcode scanning at various stages of the supply chain allows for efficient sorting, routing, and delivery of packages. This technology enhances transparency, reduces errors, and facilitates seamless coordination across the transportation network.

5. Libraries

Barcodes have transformed library operations, facilitating efficient circulation and inventory management of books and other materials. Each item in a library is labelled with a barcode, allowing for quick and accurate check-in, check-out, and inventory control. Barcode scanning automates the borrowing and returning process, minimizing manual effort and reducing errors. Libraries can also utilize barcodes for cataloguing and organizing their collections, making it easier for patrons to locate specific materials. With the serialization of books, counting and reconciliation processes has become easy and seamless.

6. Document Management

Barcodes has applications in document management systems, enabling accurate tracking, organization, and retrieval of important documents. By affixing barcodes to documents, businesses can categorize and index them electronically. Barcode scanning allows for quick identification and retrieval of specific documents, eliminating the need for manual searching and enhancing productivity in document-intensive environments.

7. Asset Tracking

Barcodes are widely used for asset tracking in industries such as manufacturing, warehousing, and IT. By labelling assets with barcodes, businesses can track the location, maintenance history, and other relevant information of equipment and property. Barcode scanning enables efficient inventory audits, asset tracking, and preventive maintenance scheduling, improving operational efficiency and reducing the risk of asset loss or misplacement.

8. Event Ticketing

Barcodes have revolutionized event ticketing systems, providing secure and efficient ticket validation and entry management. Barcoded tickets, whether printed or displayed on mobile devices, can be scanned at entry points to verify their authenticity and grant access to events. Barcode scanning ensures smooth and organized admission processes, reduces the risk of fraudulent tickets, and enhances overall event security.

9. Travel and Hospitality:

- **Boarding passes and luggage tags:** Barcodes expedite airport check-in and baggage handling, enhancing passenger experience and security.
- **Event ticketing:** Simplify access control and ticket validation at concerts, conferences, and other events with barcode-based tickets.
- **Hotel room keys:** Eliminate physical keys by using barcodes on smart phones for contactless room access, improving convenience and security.

Chapter Case Study
Barcodes Streamlining Blood Banks across the Nation

The American Red Cross faced a critical challenge–ensuring the efficiency and safety of its blood donation and distribution system. Manual tracking of blood units posed risks of errors, delays, and potential product loss.

The Red Cross implemented a comprehensive barcode system across its facilities. Blood units received unique barcodes upon donation, allowing for:

- **Real-time tracking:** Each scan recorded location, temperature, and expiry date, minimizing human error and ensuring optimal storage conditions.
- **Efficient processing:** Staff quickly verified donor eligibility and blood compatibility with barcode scans, speeding up processing and distribution.
- **Inventory management:** Barcode data streamlined inventory control, optimizing blood distribution to hospitals in need.
- **Reduced waste:** Real-time data insights helped predict demand and prevent expired blood units from reaching hospitals.

Impact
- **Reduced errors:** Barcode implementation significantly reduced manual data entry errors, improving patient safety and blood quality.
- **Faster response times:** Blood delivery to hospitals became faster and more efficient, aiding crucial medical interventions.
- **Increased donations:** Improved efficiency encouraged more blood donations due to streamlined processes and transparency.

- **Cost savings:** The Red Cross saved millions annually through reduced waste, optimized distribution, and minimized errors.

Key learning's for Novice Business Owners:

Barcodes can significantly improve efficiency and safety in industries beyond retail, like healthcare. Real-time data insights provided by barcodes enable better decision-making and resource allocation. Choosing the right barcode solution and training staff are crucial for successful implementation.

Conclusion

Barcodes have diverse applications beyond retail, revolutionizing operations across industries such as healthcare, manufacturing, transportation, libraries, document management, asset tracking, and event ticketing.

It is important to note that each of the usages highlighted above would require specially designed software or ERP to enable the integration of barcodes and its usage. There are already made packages that can be used depending on the industry of need. For instance, in the areas of asset labelling, Deloitte has a package with IBM Maximo that many entities use. The IBM Maximo itself is used by many organisations even though other prefer in-house developed packages.

By leveraging barcode technology, businesses in these sectors can improve efficiency, accuracy, and overall operational performance. The versatility and benefits of barcodes make them indispensable tools for enhancing processes, enabling traceability, and driving productivity in various contexts.

11.

The Future of Barcodes and Emerging Barcode Technologies: A Crystal Ball for Novice Business Owners

While the ordinary barcode might seem like a relic of the past, its future is surprisingly bright and brimming with innovation. For novice business owners, understanding these advancements can be like holding a crystal ball, offering a glimpse into how barcodes will transform your operations and customer experience.

Beyond the Stripes: Evolving Barcode Landscape
Remember the days of bulky scanners struggling to read pixelated 1D barcodes? Today, we're in the era of 2D barcodes like QR codes, capable of storing a wealth of information – URLs, product details, even marketing messages. Imagine scanning a QR code on a product label to instantly access its nutritional information, customer reviews, or even a personalized discount offer.

Smarter Scanning: Technology Takes the Lead

The future of barcode scanning is intelligent and omnidirectional. Consider "smart tunnels" that scan items at high speeds regardless of their orientation, streamlining inventory management and checkout processes in stores. Image-based recognition technologies are also on the rise, allowing barcode readers to identify products based on their appearance, even if the code is damaged or obscured.

Beyond Products: The Rise of Invisible Barcodes

Barcodes are no longer limited to physical products. Digimarc, for example, embeds invisible codes directly into product images or packaging, allowing for seamless authentication, anti-counterfeiting measures, and even interactive experiences. Imagine scanning a magazine cover to unlock exclusive content or a product image on social media to access its purchase link.

Merging Worlds: The Barcode-IoT Connection

The Internet of Things (IoT) is weaving its magic into the barcode world. Imagine temperature-sensitive food items equipped with tiny RFID tags, triggering alerts if they deviate from optimal storage conditions. Or, consider smart shelves that automatically track inventory levels and trigger restocking orders–all thanks to embedded barcodes and their connection to the IoT ecosystem.

The Customer at the Centre: A Personalized Experience

The future of barcodes is all about empowering customers. Imagine scanning a QR code on a restaurant menu to personalize your order with dietary restrictions or allergies. Or, think of scanning a code in a store to access product reviews, compare prices with online retailers, or even initiate a virtual shopping assistant for personalized recommendations.

Embracing the Future: A Roadmap for Novice Business Owners

As a novice business owner, navigating this evolving landscape can feel overwhelming. But fear not! Here's your roadmap:

- **Start with the basics:** Implement basic 1D and 2D barcoding for inventory management and point-of-sale systems.
- **Stay informed:** Keep an eye on emerging barcode technologies and their potential applications in your industry.
- **Experiment strategically:** Start small with pilot projects to test new barcode solutions and assess their impact on your business.
- **Embrace partnerships:** Collaborate with technology providers and consultants to guide

your barcode journey.

The future of barcodes is not just about technology; it's about creating a more efficient, personalized, and engaging experience for your customers. By embracing these advancements, you can ensure your business stays ahead of the curve and thrives in the ever-evolving world of commerce.

As a novice business owner, remember that the key is in understanding your specific needs and challenges. Do not be afraid to seek expert advice and tailor your barcode strategy to your unique business goals.

www.ingramcontent.com/pod-product-compliance
Lightning Source LLC
Chambersburg PA
CBHW071303050326
40690CB00011B/2511